SCHOLASTIC INC.
New York Toronto London Auckland Sydney

ISBN 0-590-46622-4

 Published by Scholastic Inc.,
by arrangement with Lorimar Telepictures Corporation,
c/o Warner Bros. Consumer Products, 4000 Warner Boulevard,
Burbank, CA 91522.

Book designed by Ursula Herzog

12 11 10 9 8 7 6 5 4 3 2 1 3 4 5 6 7 8/9

Printed in the U.S.A. 08

First Scholastic printing, February 1993

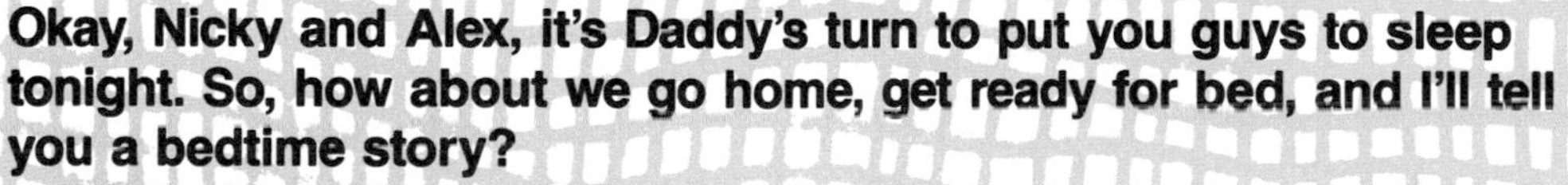

Okay, Nicky and Alex, it's Daddy's turn to put you guys to sleep tonight. So, how about we go home, get ready for bed, and I'll tell you a bedtime story?

What should it be? *Jack and the Beanstalk*? Naah. I always thought "fee fi fo fum" was dumb! *Snow White?* Naah. I don't want to scare you guys off applesauce forever! I know, I'll get out my snapshot album and tell you the coolest story of all — the story of your very own family.

This album of mine is full of pictures of all the people who live in this house — me, your mom, Uncle Danny, Cousin D.J., Cousin Stephanie, Cousin Michelle, and our pal Joey. If we look real hard, I'll bet we can find a couple of pictures of you guys, too!

Let's see . . . well, here's a good place to start. This was taken the very first day I came to live with your Uncle Danny. It was a happy-sad time. My big sister, your Aunt Pam, had just died, and I moved in to help Uncle Danny take care of their girls — D.J., Stephanie, and Michelle.

Uncle Danny needed a lot of help so he asked his pal Joey Gladstone to move in, too! We became one big happy family — eventually.

One Big Happy Family!

It took a while for me to get used to living in such a *full house*. When I first moved in your Uncle Danny gave me Michelle's old room. I couldn't believe how *frilly* it was! But, I quickly gave the place some ooh-soo-cool Jesse personality! The first thing I did was hang up a life-size photo of my idol, the King of Rock 'n' Roll — Elvis Presley!

Your Cousin D.J. was plenty mad when I moved in. Suddenly *she* was forced to share a room with Stephanie! D.J. moved out to the garage instead. It took a lot of talking and *twenty bucks* for me to convince her to move back in. Now don't you two get any ideas about getting easy money from me. I've learned a lot about talking to kids since then!

Here's something I bet you two didn't know — I changed a *lot* of diapers before you two came along! That's because your Cousin Michelle was just a little bitty baby when I first came to live here.

D.J. and Stephanie are two puppy lovers. D.J.'s a great baby-sitter, too, even if she won't sit on Saturday nights! But that's okay, 'cause Stephanie will — at least until *she* starts dating!

Me and My Michelle

I'm close to all three of your cousins. But Michelle and I have a special kind of relationship. I've been telling her all my hopes and dreams before she could answer back.

She kind of flips for me, too!

For a little kid, Michelle's got great fashion sense.

You wouldn't believe the crazy things I've done to keep this kid laughing — playing a clown on her birthday was just one of those things.

The Cutest Doggone Pet!

Here's another member of our family, Comet. That's right, Nicky, *doggie*!

Hey, D.J., wanna dance?

Looks like the girls are playing *ruff*!
Am I funny or what?

Everyone around here makes jokes about my hair, but the truth is, they're all jealous. And as soon as you guys grow some hair, I'll show you the proper way to mousse, massage, and comb it, so it looks as good as Daddy's. In this picture you can see that my hair was *long*.

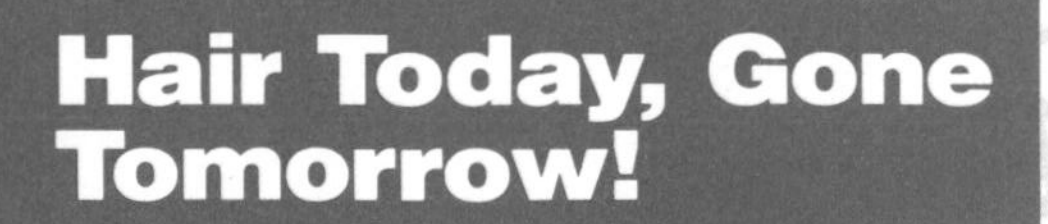

Hair Today, Gone Tomorrow!

Then your Cousin Stephanie got the great idea of playing beauty parlor! Ouch! I can still feel the pain when she snipped off that lock of hair!

But I got used to short hair. It was sort of "hair today, gone tomorrow"! Besides, even with short hair, I looked terrific!

Here's short-haired Daddy with baby Michelle. This is one of my favorite pictures.

No one's ever lonely around here. Because there are a *lot* of people living in our house. Sometimes, we all get on each other's nerves. But one thing's for sure — it's never boring! Just look at this . . . don't ask me what wacky Joey is doing here! What a comedian!

Only *I* can turn a completely geeky game like golf into a cool sport!

It's One Full House!

You can usually find Uncle Danny in the kitchen — making sure he can see himself in his dishes! Just call him "Mr. Clean."

Helmets are cool. They protect your head . . . and your hair!

Just call me Mighty Dad!

Ask any of your cousins, there's no uncle like an Uncle Jesse! I've always been there for the girls — and they've always been there for me.

If you think we've got a full house now, you should've been here when the girls wanted to keep *all* these puppies. No way! We returned the puppies to the owner of the mother dog. But, we kept one very special puppy — Comet!

Sometimes you'll find this extra person kind of roaming our halls. She's Kimmy Gibbler, D.J.'s best friend. She doesn't really live with us — she just hangs out here, all the time! Go home, Kimmy!

Wanna Be Like the King!

It took a while, but my music career is really starting to take off! I want to be as famous as Elvis Presley. All right, maybe I'll never be as popular as the King, but I can dream, can't I?

Check out this trio! Doo wop, doo wop!

My band plays my kind of music. It's good old fashioned rock and roll — the kind of stuff Elvis would have been proud of!

Here's Cousin Michelle sittin' in with the band!

And here's D.J. getting private tutoring on how to play the guitar. There's nothing like learning from a pro!

This concert was a family affair. Check out who's singing backup for me!

Here are some of my all-time favorite photos. I've been saving them to use on the cover of one of my albums — or a *big* poster. Which one do you like best, Alex? How about you Nicky?

Rock 'n' Roll Pin-ups!

Fender

Believe it or not, Uncle Danny knew your mom before I did! Before she had you two, your mom and Uncle Danny worked together on the TV show *Wake Up San Francisco*.

Beautiful Becky!

I remember the first time I laid eyes on her — beautiful Becky Donaldson — all I could say was "Ooooh, *have mercy*!"

Your mom and I were actually engaged twice. The first time, we eloped and were going to get married in Las Vegas. But Becky left me at the altar. I guess the time just wasn't right.

I didn't give up on her, though. It took a lot of courting, but eventually I convinced your mom to become Mrs. Rebecca Katsopolis. Bet you can't say that three times fast! What am I saying? You guys can't say *anything* three times fast!

She Loves Me, She Loves Me Not!

Getting Becky to agree to marry me was easy compared to planning the wedding! Would you believe your mother wanted to have some hokey hee haw wedding in Nebraska?

Now me, I wanted to have the wedding at Elvis Presley's mansion, Graceland! After all, I look so cool in shades.

After a lot of discussion, we decided to get married right here in San Francisco. Now I know you guys weren't on the guest list or anything, but don't be insulted. You weren't even born yet!

We have tons of wedding pictures to show you, though. Just take a look.

Our Wedding Album!

Would you believe I almost missed our wedding! I had this great idea to go skydiving right before the ceremony. At least it seemed like a good idea at the time. But I got sort of "hung up." I was *so* late for the ceremony, I had to get to the church on a bus!

We got married in an old church. It was really traditional — with a choir and everything! Michelle was our flower girl.

The minister asked, "Do you, Becky, take Jesse to be your lawfully wedded husband?"

I could hardly believe my ears when she said, "I do!"

We walked down the aisle together as the new Mr. and Mrs. Katsopolis.

Everyone gathered around your mom and me for our first dance as husband and wife.

Hey, Becky, don't smash that cake in my hair!

The reception was a wild time!

Mommy and me — our wedding portrait.

After the honeymoon, your mom and I came back to live in our own apartment in Uncle Danny's house. It was really romantic.

A Double Surprise!

Then your mom had a little surprise for me. She told me we were going to have a baby. At least we thought it was *a* baby . . .

I'll never forget the time the doctor told me there was going to be *two* of you guys! Have mercy! I was never so scared in my life! It was one thing to be responsible for one little baby. But two? Still, deep down, I knew that together, your mom and I could handle anything.

I don't know if you guys remember this, but I talked to you the whole time you were in your mommy's tummy. . . . Was that a yawn, Alex?

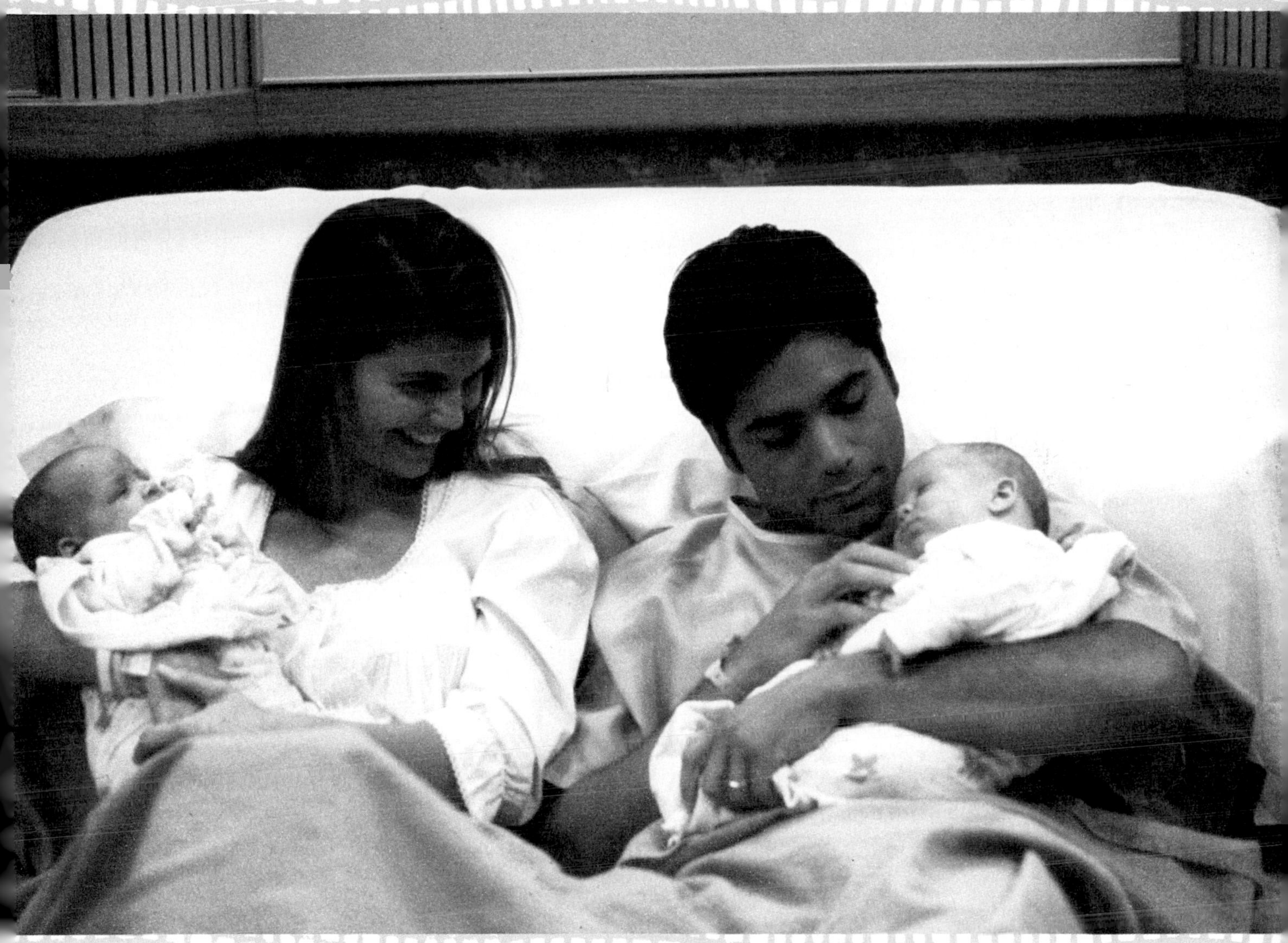

The day you little fellows were born was the greatest day your mom and I have ever shared! It was also the end of either of us ever getting any sleep! Don't both of you ever feel like sleeping late on a Sunday morning?

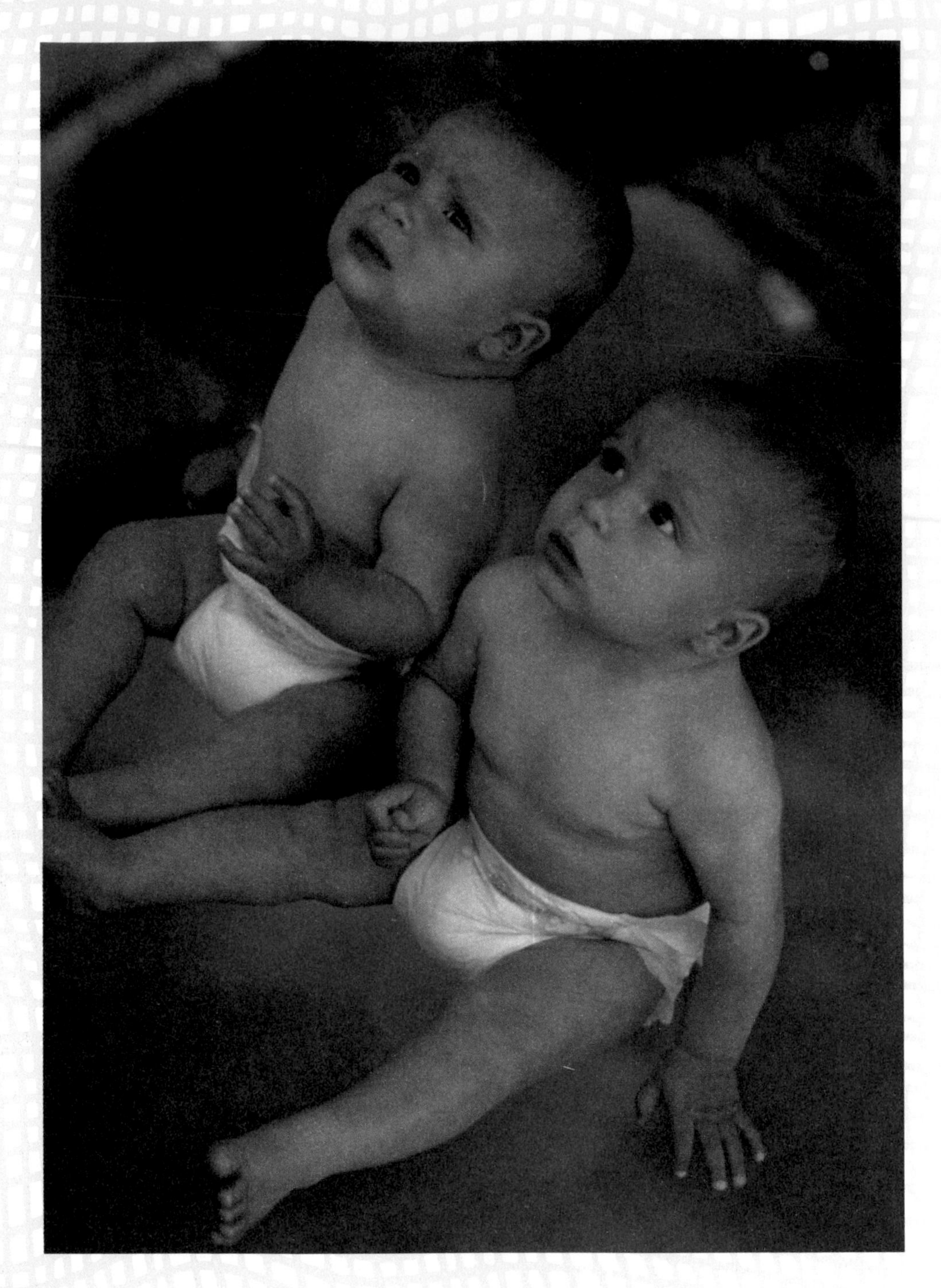

You two are the most handsome babies in the world. Now I know lots of dads say that, but they're wrong and I'm right!

Of course, it's not easy being the father of twins. Keeping track of both of you at once is tough! Just going food shopping with you is an adventure.

But twice the work also means twice the love. And your mom and I sure do love you!

I wouldn't trade my time with my twin boys for anything in the world — except a little shut-eye. So how about it, Nickster and Big Alex? Let's say night-night. Okay? Pretty please? . . . Sleep tight!